Bitcoin
Picture Concepts

Niel Ryan

DEDICATION

Satoshi Nakamoto – Creator of Bitcoin.

CONTENTS

ACKNOWLEDGMENTS

Thanks to all of the amazing creativity of the tens of thousands of people working tirelessly to develop Bitcoin.

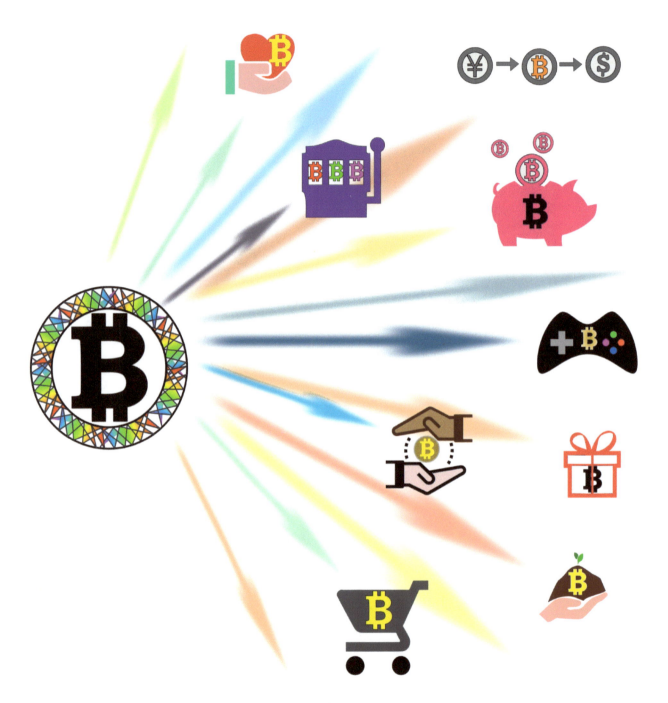

14Uf75HT4r6p8bC13SiYjvstZnyvhTtS3m

₿0.001

14Uf75HT4r6pBbC13SiYjvstZnyvhTtS3m

$100

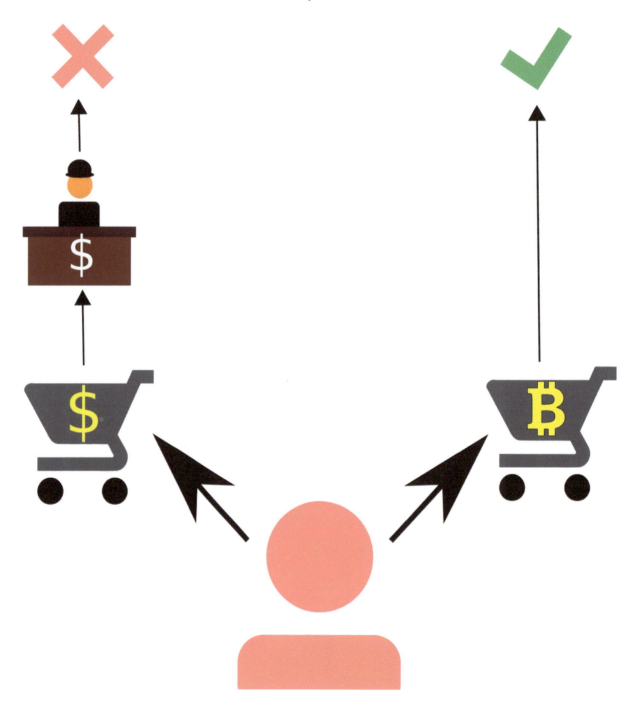

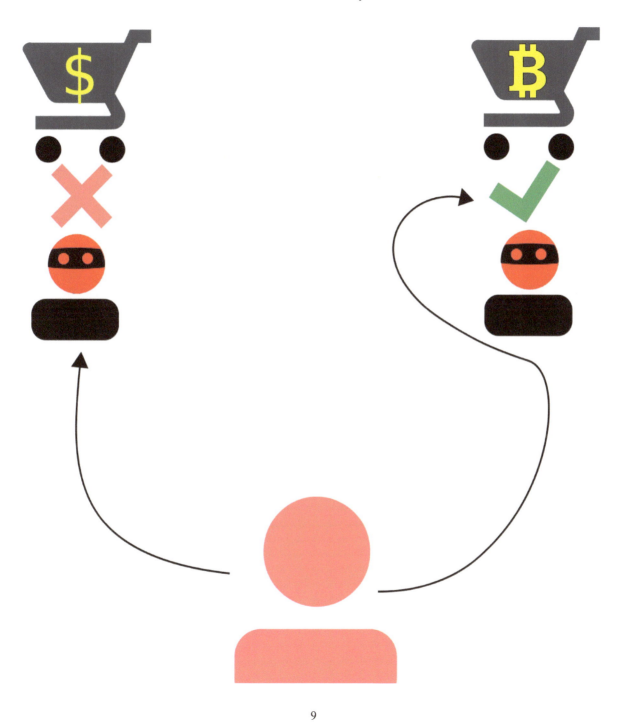

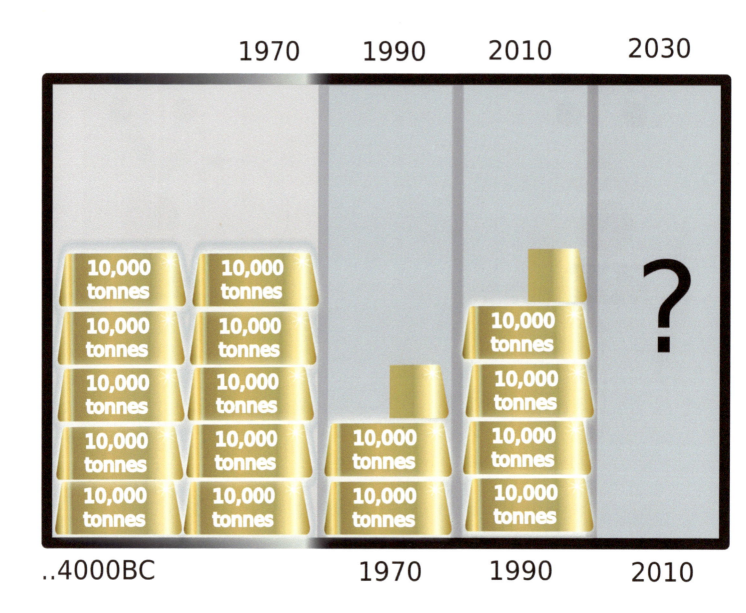

Bitcoin Picture Concepts

1970 **1990** **2010** **2030**

?

1,000,000,000,000
$

1,000,000,000,000
$
1,000,000,000,000
$
1,000,000,000,000
$
1,000,000,000,000
$

1,000,000,000,000
$
1,000,000,000,000
$
1,000,000,000,000
$
1,000,000,000,000
$
1,000,000,000,000
$

1,000,000,000,000
$
1,000,000,000,000
$
1,000,000,000,000
$
1,000,000,000,000
$
1,000,000,000,000
$

1792 **1970** **1990** **2010**

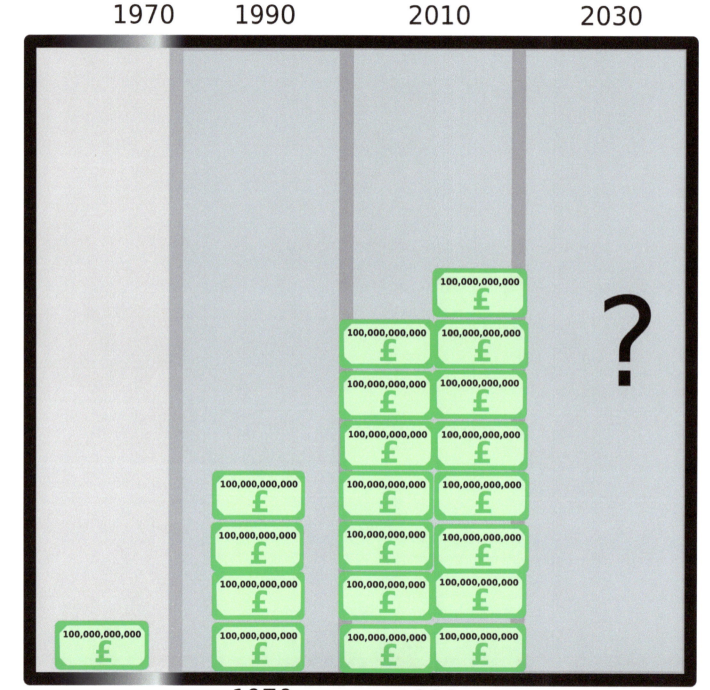

Bitcoin Picture Concepts

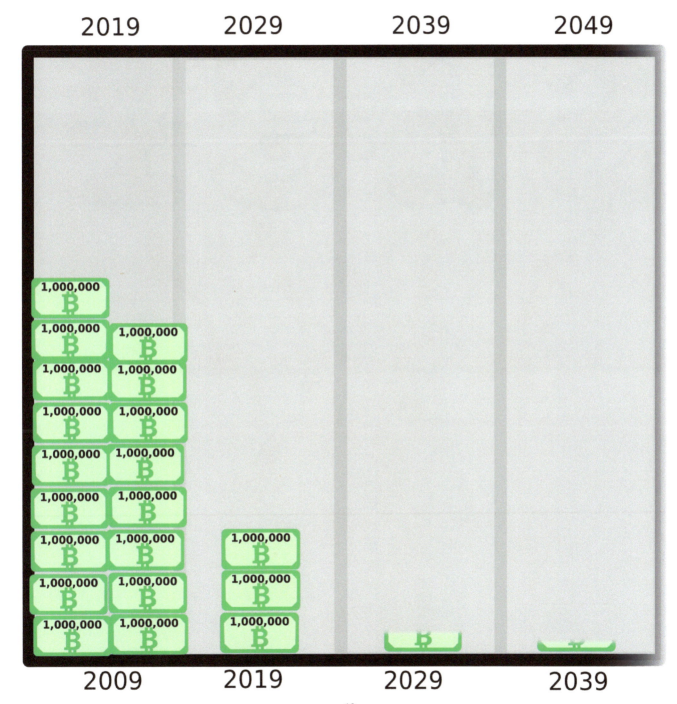

13

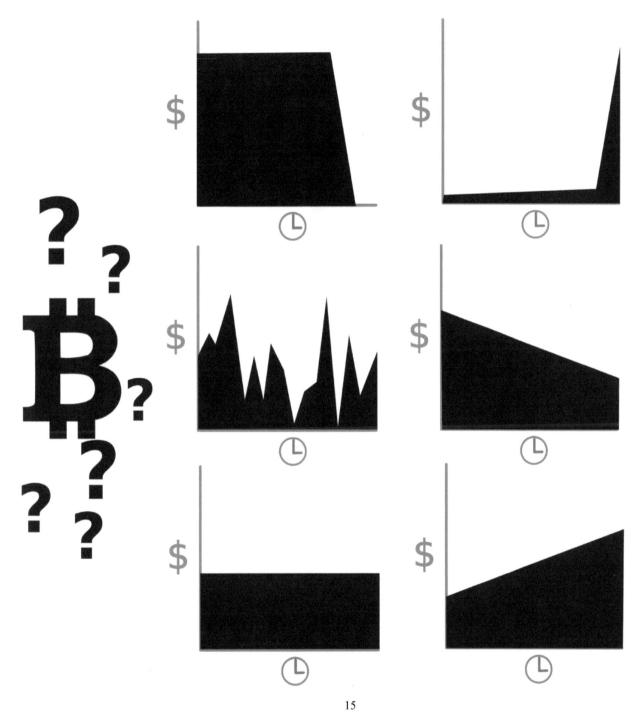

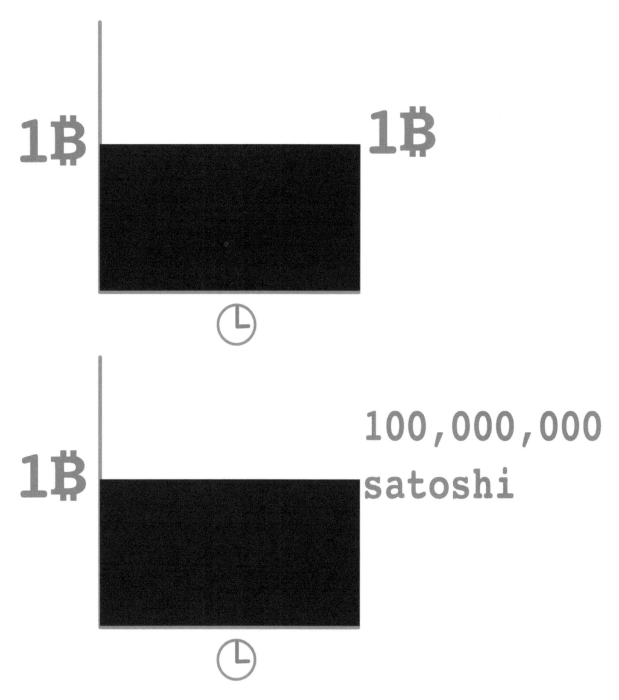

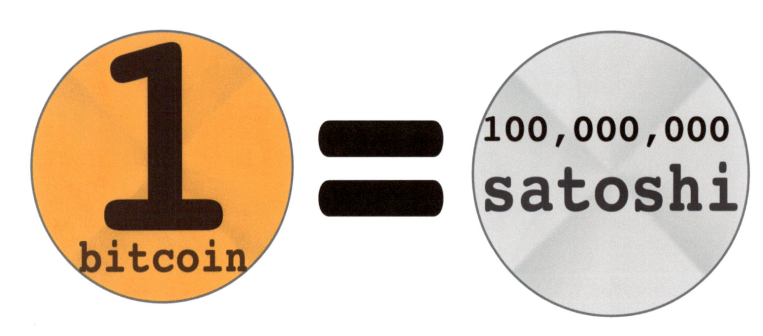

Niel Ryan

ABOUT THE AUTHOR

Niel Ryan is a technology evangelist, traveler and teacher. Having lived in England, China, Kazakhstan and The Netherlands. He writes books that make the understanding of our lives easier. His philosophy of teaching and presenting information is that it must accessible to anyone, no matter what their native language or literacy level.

www.ingramcontent.com/pod-product-compliance
Lightning Source LLC
Chambersburg PA
CBHW041425050326
40689CB00002B/656